I AM NOT YOUR DOORMAT

Emily Holwadel

This book is dedicated to everyone that has ever believed in me. I believe in you too.

Anomie

What is inner peace?
When everyone is really a beast.
I can practice human teachings
But I'll still lack what I am seeking.
Maybe the darkest parts of me know
The epiphany I need to undergo.
I am no more human than a cannibal.
We are all animals.
What is it without adrenaline release?
A human-made disease?

Shy Away

Inside my shell, I can't hear the ocean.
I listen to the sound of sweet daydreams.
Life is just passing me by while I hide.
Any inch out, shows my vulnerabilities.
I don't want the world to see me so soft.
So I stay inside of my colorful shell.

Learning to Ride the Waves

My mood swings are waves crashing below my surface.
Internal ocean shifting
From sparkling turquoise to midnight blue.
Characterized by capriciousness.
In my eyes, you can either see me drowning
Or riding my waves with a smile.
I'll try to choke back the waves,
But avoiding the waves only causes them to grow.
I can't swim
But I am determined to learn how to surf.
I won't allow my internal ocean to swallow me whole.

Lifelong Learner

Life begins to split off into parallels.
Moments of deja vu in all of my inner hells.
I am back nervously scrambling my locker
Or hiding from my stalker.
Beneath all of these instances
I am infinite.
These images meet at a convergence.
Causing my personal emergence.
I'm learning all of those lessons
Not taught in any class sessions.
I tried to reinvent myself, but I never finished
Until I realized I am a new person every minute.
I can't waste those actions
Or social transactions.
I don't feel like I've grown much
All of these years, cowering in fear and such.
But I am facing it now.
I will defeat it somehow.

Creativity

Ideas are fleeting light bulbs.
It will shine for a few seconds
And then begin to flicker.
Write those ideas down
Before they burn out.
Let your ideas ignite the midnight oil
And awaken your deepest thoughts.
Keep your extra ideas in the junk drawer
Next to the ketchup packets and the spare hardware.
You never know when an idea will come in handy.
I'm practically a packrat of ideas.
Layers of post-its notes
Ripped scraps of paper
And crayon scribblings on receipts.

Time to Introvert

It became easier to be home alone.
I found new skills I needed to hone.
Poetry isn't written in company.
Over my shoulder, the words come out clumsily.
Writing books
Can easily warrant strange looks.
Writers curse
After each draft, especially the first.
You can be afraid someone will see you
And try to get through.
Poetry can reveal your tears.
It's like drowning in your deepest fears.
Don't write poems unless you're alone.
Your words need to be your own.
Not borrowed.
Poetry is a lonely road.

Socially Awkward

Social cues and norms confuse me.
Like who are you supposed to invite to your wedding?
It's always better to invite too many people
Then to leave someone out.
I always wonder if a forgotten old friend
Holds a grudge for never receiving an invitation.
Is it socially acceptable to list everyone
That has ever influenced you
In your book's acknowledgments?
Or should I trim the list down?
I don't even know who to ask
Because it will warrant a strange look.
I feel like my social skills
Should have advanced more by now
But they haven't.
Over break, I searched for an app to help
But none were created
To help the socially awkward.
I'm clueless in picking up subtle hints.
I even miss the most overt signs.
Sometimes it feels like I need a translator
To make sense of what other people say.

Overly Religious

Anxiety
Is my deity.
My mind is its temple
Worship is simple.
I give it my all.
I am at my anxiety's beck and call.

Anxiety

It's intertwined in all of my tales,
The voice inside my head telling me I will fail.
It's the third wheel in all of my relationships,
From birth, it's been attached to my hip.
Anxiety fucks me harder than anyone else can.
Until I can't even stand.
If you look closely,
It's in my selfies, behind me mostly.

My Soundtrack

I love all of those hype men.
They are like my soul's kin.
Lil Jon can narrate the story of my life
Say "Yeahhh" if you're filled with strife
Anxiety is the lead singer of my band.
It can scream louder than I can.
It can make the whole room shake.
It sure knows how to take,
"Shots Shots Shots"
At me.

My Uniform

Charcoal heather gray sweaters
Long enough to swallow my form.
Big black motorcycle boots with buckles.
Navy blue tank top with paint stains.
Ripped jeans with ink smeared doodles.
Hoodies used to strike me as boring.

Young Adult Rebel

Teen angst is relevant more in my late twenties.
It never resonated with me at the age when it's trendy.
I don't want to simply survive and live.
I want to conquer my life and make it my own.
It's an uphill battle.
Structure can feel like a shackle.
Somehow this isn't the life I always imagined.
But I will create a new life full of passion.

Grow

I always imagine driving off into the sunset.
But I haven't yet.
I drive back to the office,
Leaving my daydreams in my pockets.
Close enough for comfort.
Awaiting the day, I run for it.
I don't shoot for the stars,
Because in retrospect, that's not all that far.
I shoot for the unknown.
Because that's the only way I'll ever feel grown.

Night Shift

There's nothing romantic about a 9 to 5.
At 5, I don't even feel alive.
Take me back to when
The night air would gently kiss my hand.
All that feeling of relief
Is now replaced by grief.

Seasonal Depression

The spring winds make me feel normal.
I'm fine again until fall.
As the leaves decay,
I feel myself gradually fade away.
My skin lacks its original pigment.
I am hell sent.

Photography

If I photograph it right,
I'll capture my eyes in the correct light.
My smile doesn't seem to match
The other half.
Makeup can hide flaws,
But lipstick won't give me a real smile.

Facial Expressions

I can feel emotions in my eyes.
There's a certain look of hunger
In being tired.

Lack of Inspiration

My paintbrush no longer lives in my hand.
It feels like a stranger.
I can't seem to find the right colors.
To capture what is going on inside my head.
The colors are muddy and ruined.

Writer's Block

I have not written in a week,
Something in it makes my soul weak.
My moods have darkened.
A new journey for me to embark on.
My eyes no longer match my smile.
There's no energy left for me to rile.
Scrunch my hair in the waves.
Hide my face, so I no longer have to be brave.

Why?

I thought I had achieved some of my biggest goals.
I graduated from college.
I got married to the man I love.
I had two beautiful daughters.
But now I'm left scratching my head.
Why am I not happy?
I don't know when it shifted.
One minute I was on top of the world,
Smile shining,
Confident,
Independent diva.
Holding my head high.
Jokes and giggles.
Then it all faded away.

Antidepressants

Depression doesn't accept happiness coins.
Spending my paycheck is also not a cure.
There was never really a breaking point.
It can't be simplified in just one moment.
It's more complex than that.
It would be easier if I was more straightforward.
But I can't just travel from point A to point B.
I like to frequent point Z
And point Y has the best tacos.
But again, I digress.
How am I supposed to ever make progress?
I just woke up one day
With a deep sadness that I couldn't escape.
It enveloped me and forced me to face it.

Music Therapy

I'll listen to the music
And hope it takes me someplace I can heal.
Other artists know exactly how I feel.
The intensity beams.
What if it's more than depression?
I can be my case study.
I don't want anyone to look directly in my eyes.

Defined by Disorder

If I take away the mental illness,
What will be left?
Empty thoughts and a blank mind?
The anxiety gives me energy.
Proper paranoia.
It's a motivator.
They ask in interviews,
What's your biggest motivation
But no one ever says,
"It's my anxiety breathing down my neck."
No one ever says,
"It's so my depression doesn't win."
They are fighting over me.
I don't know what has come over me.
I look in the mirror
And I don't even recognize myself.
What am I doing?
I hope no one notices
I'm not okay,
Because it's too painful to talk about the issues.

Seek Help

Food is now tasteless.
But I can't say I am blameless.
I thought I could fight it on my own.
Thought it was showing me the skills I needed to hone.
I didn't realize I would become so lost.
It wasn't worth the cost.
Next time I'll be smarter
And know it's not about working harder.
If I can write it all down,
Maybe, the old me will be found.

Buried Emotions

Cataloging emotions
Requires utter devotion.
The categories are unclear,
Facing feelings invokes fear.
It's easy to turn to repression,
But it's not the cure to depression.
I'll place my feelings on the shelf,
So I don't lose myself.

Taking Back Me

I am reclaiming myself from the abyss.
My struggles aren't subjects to reminisce.
I'd honestly rather avoid talking,
But the silence only left me falling.
Arms crossed, I am ready to ready to face it all.
Even if it requires a complete overhaul.
I am not going to tremble when I speak.
I will embrace what is bleak.
I deserve to move forward.
My mind doesn't need to be tortured.
The flashbacks are still in the back,
Patiently waiting for me to crack.
There's reasoning behind all of my hesitations.
I was chained by expectations.

UNPACKING MY BAGGAGE

My Ex's Apartment

I don't know if I am ready to talk about the roaches.
Their creepy-crawly legs were approaching.
Filthy skeletons stained on the walls.
Suffocating baby powder lining the halls.
He slept on the floor with the creatures.
The voracious eaters.
Is this what it feels like to be in jail?
His laziness created an environment for them to dwell.

Losing Virginity

It was a murder scene.
It felt like a butcher knife carving inside of me.
I bit down on a pillow,
And followed orders like a dog.
It would be dramatic to say I was dying,
But the pain was more intense than childbirth.
Wounded for days.
It instilled fear in me.

My Chess Opponent

He always said relationships were like chess
Continuously predicting the next five moves.
But in chess, it's an equal playing field.
I didn't know the rules
And I was the only piece against his full lineup.
I didn't want to play his game.
I forfeited all turns
And then became stuck in a corner.
Checkmate.

City Dump Records

Men always try to make themselves
More interesting than they really are at first.
They'll give you their lame-ass mixtape,
That they aren't even on.
Their "freestyle" doesn't even rhyme.

Pajama Bottoms

I had a personal fashion police.
No makeup was allowed out of the house,
Or he would ask who I was trying to impress.
My bottoms couldn't be too tight
Or show my slender figure.
Baggy sweat pants were ideal.
Dresses and skirts were off-limits.
I couldn't even look feminine.
T-shirts that were two sizes too large were always safe.

Road Rage

Aggressive driving was never in my nature,
But I learned to understand road rage.
Those moms with the honking horns
Might have a date with their husbands' fist
If they arrive late.
Traffic delays made me anxious.

I'm Not Allowed to Drive on the Road Less Traveled

I take a picture of the timeclock,
To prove when I leave work.
I have to arrive home at the same time each night.
Or there will be questions and another fight.
He will criticize whatever road I take,
Even the interstate.
"You drove past 25th street to see your boyfriend's house."
"You stopped at the stoplight too long, what were you doing?"
It comes to the point
Where I don't want to drive anywhere except off of a bridge.

Interrogation

Bring in the rectangular card table
And the bright desk lamp to shine truth.
I'm ready for your latest interrogation.
There's no good cop and bad cop,
We both know there's no justice.
Him: "Where were you at this time?"
Me: "At work."
Him: "Who were you with?"
Me: "My coworkers."
Him: "What were you doing?"
Me: "Unloading the truck."
Him: "Oh, you were fucking your boss. You slut! I knew it."
It doesn't matter what I say.
The interrogations always end the same way.

Losing Me

You tell me guys are more visual.
But I want to be an individual.
I don't feel like myself,
And sometimes it feels like hell.
Do I have to lose parts of me to be
Part of your whole?
What's next?
Selling my soul?

Diamond

Dreams mined out of my mind.
Until there was no treasure left to find.
Pearls of wisdom lost all of their glimmer.
My life grew dimmer.
My mind became a piece of coal.
It felt like I had lost my soul.
I was a sleeping dragon
Waiting to awaken.

It's Not Like the Movies

For someone with no criminal record,
I sure have taken a lot of lie detector tests.
It feels like a routine medical exam,
Blood pressure and pulse checked.
The test would give him faith for a couple of days.
But then he'd be back to his old antics.
"You're cheating on me." He would say.
Accused of bribing the proctor,
Finding language loopholes,
And tricking the test.

Anonymous Like Banksy

I feel like the graffiti on the concrete wall.
Cheap spray paints
Peeling murals.
I'm just waiting until it's time for me to fall.
Maybe with all of this around me,
I am becoming toxic too.

Questions

People asked why you allowed it,
But it wasn't a case of permission.
Each time you left, he found you.
Standing behind your car,
You couldn't escape.
He showed up at your school,
Knew the room numbers to all of your classes.
Always in the parking lot in the spot next to you.
He'd show up to your parents' house,
Hoping for a compromise.
There wasn't an easy way out.
Besides, there were the finances.

Paging Doctor Dumbass

Dr. Dumbass prepares me for my exam.
No need to put on gloves
Because I am his property.
My female anatomy has to be checked
For any flaws.
He invades me with his fingers
Always finding problems with my body.
He says I am bigger than yesterday,
Like I've been stretched by someone else.
But I remain untouched except by him.
I've grown to hate my body.
It betrays me by not fitting into his narrow guidelines.
Doctor Dumbass isn't a gynecologist,
Or even a doctor at all.
He's my boyfriend.

Expired Innocence

They always say you're sweet
Until you reach a certain age.
All of the sweetness inside has expired
And became bitter.
He does his best to trap you in a cage.
Not even free when you're alone.

The Night Before I Was Kicked Out Of My Parents' House

Raindrops beat the windshield loudly,
A reminder of the tears that hit my cheeks.
I wished I could have windshield wipers on my glasses.
It was rough
Constantly wiping them off.
All the rain and streetlights
Distorted the vision in the windshield.
As the thunder boomed,
I wished I could have that kind of power.
I was more like lightning.
If you looked long enough at me,
You could see flashes of anger and pain.
Most people never bothered to look.
Like lightning, I felt this part of my life
Would only last a short time.
I felt the abuse would merely be fleeting.

He Eats Enough Donuts to be a Cop

I'm not paranoid about big brother,
Because I've been watched by another.
I have experience
Under surveillance.
Security camera pointed at my bed,
I wish it would've all been in my head.
Late night stakeouts in my backyard.
My windows were practically barred.
He would memorize my car's miles.
I was treated like a criminal on trial.

Always Watching

I started sleeping with the lights on,
Not because I was afraid of the dark,
But to ensure maximum visibility for the camera.
I had to wear a sleeping mask to block the spotlight out.
I would've liked to have worn earplugs to block
His voice and the security camera alarm out.
I could no longer use my puffy comforter.
He always accused me of having another body under it.
My blanket had to be thin and short.
It didn't matter if I was cold.
As long as he could see, I was the only one in my bed.

Nightly Rules

Don't wake up in the middle of the night.
Don't open your eyes ever.
Don't look at the time and doze back to sleep.
Try not to breathe.
It makes it easier.
Lie there until the alarm goes off,
Until it's morning at least.
Don't pee in the middle of the night.
Don't rummage for a midnight snack.
"DON'T TOUCH YOUR PHONE."
He yelled loudly through the security camera app,
Startling me from my half-asleep thought daze.
I was not even near my phone that rested on the tripod.

Losing Pieces of Me

When your self-image becomes
Dependent on someone else,
You're doomed never to know who you are.
Don't expect yourself to grow,
If you're hiding in the dark shade,
Away from the nourishing sunlight.
Your power isn't inside anyone else,
But you.

He Doesn't Control You

He doesn't control you,
But he gives you recommendations.
Recommend this
Recommend that.
You're always wrong when you don't take his advice.
You no longer feel like you're living your own life.
He doesn't control you
But he always has to repeat his opinion
Over and over.
He says it's to make you understand,
But he always wants you to agree.
He doesn't control you
But he teases you about being a child
And you can feel it with the difference.
He doesn't control you
But you're guilty for everything he does for you.
He works at a job he hates.
And it's your fault.
He said he wants more,
But you're the only one that works for more.
He doesn't control you
But he doesn't want you to be so shy.
He wants to be the one that bosses you around.
He likes to work at the same place as you,
So he can always keep tabs.
He'll sneak over to your department,
On the other side of the factory.
He doesn't control you
But you can't talk politics and religion with him.
Because he always tries to convert you.
He doesn't control you,
But you haven't seen your parents in months
And he doesn't like it when you text your mom.
Your phone cannot ring in his presence.

He even thinks the debt collectors are side boyfriends.
He doesn't control you,
But you walk on needles around him.
One misheard word is another grievance.

He Doesn't Even Appreciate Music

I couldn't even show him the songs
I was listening to in my car.
"Hymn for the Weekend"
Made him question if I had a weekend boyfriend.
That new Taylor Swift song,
And I got asked who I was thinking about during the song.
My ears were in chains.

Attention Whore

He has to take over all of the conversations
Like an attention whore.
Your friends don't want to hear what he has to say.
He thinks if he talks louder,
That he wins the argument.
Without proof, he has to be right.
If you disagree, it will only stir a fight.
It's his hobby to humiliate you
In front of everyone you know.

Love Story

He told me I was the perfect ~~woman~~ victim
Gullible, I believed in him.
His insecurities were ~~my fault~~ ploys for control.
He was my ~~love~~ personal troll.
I felt ~~loved~~ like a maniac.
No fighting back.
I pushed him through the wall once.
Being ~~kissed~~ beat became an everyday occurrence.
I couldn't go to his house in a happy mood.
It caused him to ask me if I was with another dude.
My smiles ~~were huge~~ disappeared.
And he became the object of my ~~affection~~ fears.
I jumped through hoops to prove my innocence
I was determined to achieve blissfulness.
GPS trackers and all of my messages for him to view.
He always found a psychotic slant to construe.
Lie detector tests and cell phone security cameras,
My paparazzi, but I wasn't glamorous.
He watched me sleep every night.
Waking me up, he was never contrite.
I was prone to rage,
But that happens when you're locked in a cage.
I tried to use my fists to break free.
It was even less effective than a submissive plea.
No escape rope.
I had lost hope.

Uncomfortable

Air conditioning broken in the middle of summer.
Third trimester, I got to suffer.
No furniture for me to recline.
He found it all fine.
Gray mold grew for months on his dishes.
I wouldn't step foot in his kitchen.
I loved working twelve hour shifts.
Being away from him was a gift.
Lying is not a virtue.
But I created a fake curfew,
I was thankful for still living with my parents,
It meant not sleeping in his presence.

Dangerous Game

I still don't know if his gun was a bluff.
The barrel was never against my head.
I never saw it with my own eyes.
Anytime I wanted to leave,
A potential homicide and suicide
Was the card he played.
He claimed it was untraceable,
Stolen from the ghetto of Indianapolis.
No one would ever know.
I didn't care if he killed me,
But I didn't want to be the reason for his suicide.

Sensitivities

My neck is sensitive.
I joke about being strangled to death in a past life
Because the reality is darker.
Strangulation as a means to subdue me.
Sometimes I can still feel his hands around my neck.
It was never rough enough to leave marks,
But it was enough to let me know who was boss.
I fought back with my fists
Until I was unconscious.
I wasn't scared of death.
Secretly, I wished he would go too far.
My life ending meant
I would no longer have to be with him.

Not My Name

Flat coke and watery eyes.
Clenched jaws and day-old vomit.
Bruises where they shouldn't be.
Ringing in my ears
I can still feel your hands around my thin neck.
Don't call me baby.

Pixie Cut

I'll cut off all my hair
Just to spite you.
Tell you that I like girls,
'Cuz it's easier than the truth.
Give you a girl's name
So you'll believe me.
I'll dye my hair that shade of red,
The one that makes it hurt to look at me.
I don't want to be attractive to you.

Psychological Warfare

I'm all too familiar with the concept of gaslighting.
It was his favorite method of fighting.
I'm used to feeling crazy
His manipulation made life feel hazy.

Dependable

I can't comprehend my feelings,
But I can depend on your dirty dealings.
You are poison to my brain,
The reason for my energy drain.
Yell at me until my eardrums bleed.

Take Back My Stardom

Alone, I am a shining star.
In relationships, I'm dulled.
It's not a balance or evened out.
I'm not a supernova,
Waiting to explode.
I'm fading away from being overshadowed.

Anew

Fighting back is the most challenging part.
I've already been torn apart.
I need a beginning point,
Destroy me until there's nothing left.
So I can start over.

What Does It Say About Me?

What does it say about a person,
When their apartment has no furniture
Guests sit on the floor
And he sits on a bean bag.

What does it say about a person
When he lives in a hotel
Alcohol bottles to keep his mind and body well.
He'll buy you your favorite booze,
So you won't mention what he consumes.

What does it say about a person,
When he lives with mom at twenty-six years old,
"He takes care of her." that's the excuse you're told.
He barely makes enough money for rent.
Too lazy to get off of his ass to work.

What does it say about the woman,
Attracted to these men?
Is she just as fucked up?

Remembering the Old Me

I used to make up my own holidays.
I would strut like a disco ball in the hallways.
I wish I still had that dress.
Fashion was the mode I used to express
Me, myself, and I.
Throughout the years, bold colors would amplify.
Scarves in my hair,
Accessories that had all the flair.
I'm not trying to bring back all of those styles.
Some of the outfits leave me in denial.
What's the appeal of camouflage?
It belongs in someone else's garage.

Anger

If I could breathe
My fire within
Instead of swallowing the flames
I wouldn't feel so maimed.
Release my heat
Until I feel complete.

Tarantula

I am not afraid of spiders.
And I am certainly not afraid of you.
You crawl under my skin to consume my innards.
What will you feast upon when I am none?

Running Away

Money bought me happiness.
As the breadwinner,
I gained confidence.
I knew I could financially support my family without him.
I packed a few bags.
We ran away.
I was fearless, yet afraid of everything.
My new beginning came with plenty of baggage.
Baggage that I haven't fully unpacked yet.

Lady Macbeth

Becoming clean of you
Wasn't as simple as washing you away.
The filth wasn't skin-deep,
It contaminated me within my pores.
No soap was ever deep-penetrating enough.
My soul needed to be exfoliated,
But that kind of product isn't sold in a bottle.
Since you, my body was unkempt,
I can never look at myself the same again.
Becoming clean of you
Means reclaiming my body as my own.

Don't Try To Teach Me About Art

She said "Art doesn't have to be doom and gloom."
But art isn't only sunflowers,
The yellow brushstrokes don't have to be a bright hue
The colors can be dirty and grotesque.
Art can capture ugliness.
The emotions are what make art beautiful,
Not the subject matter.
Art rose from doom and gloom.
Just like me.

Random Thoughts

Messy wavy hair,
Screaming I just don't care.
Experimenting with flavor
The root beer and its frothy texture.
Cotton candy blizzards,
And the way the snow glimmers.
Tacos with grilled steak,
I'm hoping this is not another mistake.

Make Me Small

Shrinking within myself to deal
Was never an effective way to heal.
My frame is petite,
But I'm not leaving myself vulnerable for defeat.

Shopping

Electric guitars sitting against the wall
At the dusty antique store.
I wonder about their past lives.
Were they ever on stage,
With an energetic lead singer,
Bouncing around.
Did they ever get to see the mosh pits in action?
I've forgotten what one feels like against my body,
Strumming until my fingers blister.

Undercover Heavy Metal

I like all the songs that make me
Squirm uncomfortably.
I love to see myself face the darkness.
And take a taste of it.
All of the music I listen to,
Reveals a deeper sense of me.
I like the gentle whispers to the most
Gut wrenching screams.
I just want to feel
All of the emotion
Make it come out of my pores.
I need a good cleansing.
I like the songs that make me feel guilty
Everyone is a bad person.
No one is perfect
Not even you.
I like the songs that make my jaws drop

Won't Back Down

I've always liked to do things the hard way,
To prove I can.
I'll take the long way around
And meet you at the same destination.
The scenic route is always worth it.
I'll drive my car with all the windows rolled down.
Air conditioning in a car is a waste.
We're all craving five minutes of fresh air.

Birthday Wish

For my birthday, I want a pair of boxing gloves.
I won't feel awkward punching all alone.
But just in case, you can enroll me in a class.
I swear I want to kick ass.
Sign me up for wrestling
So I can fight something besides myself.

You Can't Change Me

When you're shy,
People think that inside your shell,
You're practically play-doh.
They'll try to mold you to conform.
There's already a person inside of my shell.
So fuck you and your preconceived ideas of me.
I'll never be what you want me to be.
I'm already me.

Reclaiming Myself

I'm not going to be shy anymore
Because it doesn't match my inner core.
I need to be hardened,
Instead of being a fragile flower in a garden.
I won't be your little doll.

Eviction Notice

My anxiety no longer resides here.
Evicted without care.
Leather jackets and nose rings,
Screaming until the pain no longer stings.
Transforming process,
Learning from all of my losses.
Bleach my hair to match my damaged mind.
No logic left to find.

Self-Titled Album

I want to be more punk rock,
Maybe, tell someone to suck my imaginary cock.
Fade my hair to a pink-tinged orange.
Fight the ideas that cause me to cringe.
I'll wear my motorcycle boots in the summer.
Maybe, life will no longer be a bummer.
I'll take back my name,
Because I don't want to ever be the same.

High Road

There's an act of resistance,
In providing my sensitivities subsistence.
It would be effortless to allow myself to be blighted,
From all of the times I've been slighted.
But I was not raised to be a hellion,
I'll always choose the internal rebellion.
I will raise my fist,
I believe in creating a world where we can coexist.
I will hold my stance firm,
And fight against the norm.

Leo Rising

I'll begin to embrace those leonine traits
Without debate.
They've always been inside of me
Waiting for me to set the animal free.
I can be the quietest person in the room,
With the boldest outfit like a flower in bloom.
I won't stutter and hesitate
Because a lion is not delicate.
I'll wear my pride like a scarlet letter.
And I'll let my ambition drive me to do better.

www.ingramcontent.com/pod-product-compliance
Lightning Source LLC
Chambersburg PA
CBHW021138020426
42331CB00005B/827